BRUCE LEE'S FIGHTING METHOD

BRUCE LEE'S
FIGHTING METHOD
SKILL IN TECHNIQUES
by
BRUCE LEE and M. Uyehara

Poetry by Mike Plane

©1977 Linda Lee
All rights reserved
Printed in the United States of America
Library of Congress Catalog Card Number 77-81831

Thirty-eighth printing, 2003

ISBN 0-89750-052-0

WARNING

OHARA [] PUBLICATIONS, INCORPORATED
SANTA CLARITA, CALIFORNIA

DEDICATION

To all the friends and students of Bruce Lee

ACKNOWLEDGEMENT

Our sincere appreciation to Joe Bodner, who spent so much time in photographing and developing the film. Our appreciation also goes to those who participated in this book: Dan Inosanto and Ted Wong. They were both Bruce Lee's devoted students.

To Rainbow Publications, Inc., for the use of several photographs taken by Oliver Pang.

Introduction

This book was in the making in 1966 and most of the photographs were shot then. The late Bruce Lee intended to publish this book years ago but decided against it when he learned that martial arts instructors were using his name to promote themselves. It was quite common to hear comments like: "I taught Bruce Lee" or "Bruce Lee taught me jeet kune do." And Bruce may never have seen or known these martial artists.

Bruce didn't want people to use his name to promote themselves or their schools with false pretenses. He didn't want them to attract students this way, especially the young teens.

But after his death, his widow, Linda, felt that Bruce had contributed so much in the world of the martial arts that it would be a great loss if the knowledge of Bruce would die with him. Although the book can never replace the actual teaching and knowledge that Bruce Lee possessed, it will enhance you, the serious martial artist, in developing your skill in fighting.

Bruce always believed that all martial artists train diligently for one single purpose—to defend themselves. Whether we are in judo, karate, aikido, kung fu, etcetera, our ultimate goal is to prepare ourselves for any situation.

To train yourself for this goal, you must train seriously. Nothing is taken for granted. "You have to kick or punch the bag with concentrated efforts," Bruce used to say. "If you are going to train without the concept that this is the real thing, you are short-changing yourself. When you kick or punch the bag, you have to imagine that you are actually hitting an adversary. Really concentrating, putting 100 percent in your kicks and punches, is the only way you are going to be good."

If you have already read the first two volumes of *Bruce Lee's Fighting Method*, entitled *Self-Defense Techniques* and *Basic Training*, you are now ready to continue your lesson with this third book, *Skill in Techniques*. This book explains the ways Bruce Lee trained and the ways he developed his perfect skills. Included also are techniques in sparring and parrying. The next or final book will delve more heavily into strategy in defense and attack. Most of the photos in this book and the next have never been published before.

If you have not read *Tao of Jeet Kune Do* by Bruce Lee (Ohara Publications, Inc.), please read it. It was meant to complement this book, and the knowledge from both books will give you a full picture of Bruce's art.

Jeet Kune Do

Jeet Kune Do was founded by Bruce Lee
because he felt
the martial arts were too confined.

You can't fight in pattern he used to say
because an attack
can be baffling and not refined.

Jeet Kune Do was created by Bruce Lee
to show us
that an old art must transform.

Like the day turns to night and
night, to day
the way of fighting must also reform.

Bruce Lee developed Jeet Kune Do
but wished
he didn't have a name for it!

Because the very words, Jeet Kune Do,
already indicate
that it's another martial arts form.

Any form or style does restrict
and his belief is now in conflict.

Sources:
Tao of Jeet Kune Do by Bruce Lee
Boxing by Edwin L. Haislet

Contents

Chapter VI
Skill in Movement

SKILL IN MOVEMENT

Finesse in movement is not innate;
It has to be learned like any other skill.

Practice you must or it will deteriorate;
Like any other trait, you have to drill.

Learn to move with a shuffle of your feet,
And don't despair if you feel quite awkward.

Soon you'll be a master of deceit,
especially when moving backward and forward.

Train, train, train with great determination
and you'll be on top at your first confrontation.

Skill in Movement

Skill in movement is very important in the art of fighting. It is heavily relied upon in attack, defense, deception and conservation of energy. It is your proficiency in mobility or footwork that is contingent upon the precise distance between you and your opponent. The strategy of footwork is to take advantage of your opponent's footwork with your own. Your attack or defense may be based on the opponent's foot pattern of advancing and backing off.

When you learn his foot pattern, adjust to it. You can then press (advance) or fall back (retreat) just enough to facilitate a hit. The length of your step is coordinated to your opponent's movement. Intuition in moving forward and backward is also an intuition of when to attack and when to defend.

A skilled fighter never stays in one spot long; he is in constant motion to baffle his opponent, causing him to misjudge the distance. A moving target is harder to hit and by being in motion, you can move more quickly than from a set position.

By varying the distance and timing of your movement continuously, you can confuse your opponent. You will disturb his preparation to attack or defend, keeping him off-balance.

You must practice footwork with punching and kicking. Without footwork, the fighter is like an immobile cannon which cannot be directed at the enemy line. The speed and power of your punches and kicks depends on your nimble feet and balanced body.

A good fighter like Bruce Lee always seemed to do everything with ease, finesse and grace. He moved into his opponent and landed his blow without any effort and as easily moved out of range. He always seemed to outhit and outguess his opponent. His timing was so good that he controlled even the opponent's rhythm. He moved with assurance and coordination.

A poor fighter, on the other hand, seems to move clumsily. He can't find the correct distance, telegraphs his intentions and never seems to outthink his opponent. Instead of controlling his opponent, he lets the opponent control him.

Distance

Distance continuously changes between two skilled fighters as both attempt to seek the most advantageous position. The best idea is to stay consistently out of range of the opponent's simple punch but not too far away to deliver an attack with just a short step forward. This distance is contingent not only on your own speed and agility but also that of your opponent.

In boxing the fighters stand closer to each other than do martial artists, who utilize their feet to kick. The leg is longer than the

arm so the martial artist has a longer reach than a boxer.

In jeet kune do, there are three different distances in fighting. Generally, the longest range is employed when you don't know your opponent's prowess or his intention, as in photo 1, and you want to "feel" or "test" him out. In defense it is wiser to stay too far away instead of too close to your opponent. But in a lengthy struggle, you are only safe at a distance if you can really outclass your opponent with speed and agility in movement.

Even if you are fast, it is difficult to parry a blow if you are too near your opponent. The one who initiates the attack usually has an advantage in close quarters. But an attacker who can't properly figure out distance, will not succeed even if he is accurate, quick, has good timing and utilizes economy of movement.

Once you think that you have the "feel" of your opponent, you move closer to him, to the medium distance, as in photo 2. From this distance, you can be just out of his range and yet close enough to launch an attack. It is a safe distance if you can also apply good timing. A skillful fighter will maneuver to entice his opponent to shorten the gap or distance until the opponent is too near to avoid the trap.

This medium distance also allows you to avoid any blow by a quick retreat or a backward burst. But to use this defensive

2

strategy continuously is not always practicable because it deprives you of a counterattack or delivery of your own offense. In JKD you retreat just far enough to evade the blow but stay close enough for a counterattack.

Close distance fighting usually is a consequence of an attack or a counterattack. It is harder to defend from this distance unless you have already trapped your opponent's arms. Definitely, the advantage is to the one who initiates the attack. In close distance, as in photo 3, the fighter with the expertise of his hands will outwit the kicker.

A martial artist, unlike a boxer, needs to be alert to blows from the elbows, knees, head, etcetera, in close-fighting. IIe also has to be aware of the chance of being thrown or grappled to the ground.

In boxing, the fighters have difficulty in closing in and once they are there, it is more difficult for them to remain there. In martial arts, since the feet are employed, it is more difficult to

3

close in than in boxing. But once the fighters are in close proximity, the fight or match is over quickly because the martial artists have too many offensive tactics to use.

In close-fighting it is imperative that you immobilize your opponent's lead foot by placing yours next to his, as in photo 3. This procedure should be done automatically because at that close range, your concentration will be heavily on your hand techniques.

Lee constructed the metal bar on the wooden dummy to simulate his opponent's leg, as in photos A and B. At the outset he had to concentrate heavily on the placement of his lead foot, but after a few months, it became a natural and habitual procedure.

An in-fighting maneuver which Bruce Lee used frequently was to keep his opponent off-balance by pressing him, as in photos Y and Z. This tactic can be used against anyone, even a heavier and stronger opponent. Practice this with your partner by bending your knees slightly, placing your weight on the front foot and shoving your partner vigorously without letting up. Your feet advance with a shuffle and you use your hand and body to trap your partner's arms. The secret behind this force is to use your hips and not entirely your shoulders when you are pressing him.

Once you have your partner reeling backward, you can use your free hand to hit his body and then pin him to the ground. It is a safe maneuver because your partner cannot take the offensive. He is too off-balance to retaliate.

The better fighter is always maneuvering, trying to stay in the range that suits him best. He is just out of the opponent's attack-range and patiently waits for the right moment to close in or draw the opponent toward him. He may attack as the opponent advances or when he sees an opening while the opponent is changing his pace or position.

The attack or retreat should be rapid, penetrating and spontaneous. The opponent should not be able to predict your movement until it is too late for him to retaliate or defend. The ideal time for the attack to be delivered is when he is in stupor.

Distance is so vital that even a small mistake in range can render an attack harmless. You should launch your attack just before the opponent is at your desired distance, not after he reaches the desired range. It is like baseball, when the outfielder begins to run in the right direction even before the batter swings his bat. Or a football quarterback who throws the ball at the spot just before the end reaches it.

Y

Z

Footwork

Against a fighter who has a good sense of distance and is difficult to reach in frontal attacks, the maneuver to "bridge the gap" or to close the distance is to take a series of steps backward, progressively shortening them. Or let your opponent take the initiative as he closes the distance when he lunges at you.

If you are against a defensive fighter with a good sense of distance, advance with a series of steps, making the first step smooth and economical. A clever maneuver is to advance a step or two and then retreat, enticing the opponent to pursue. If he does, allow him to take a step or two and you can surprise him with a burst forward right into his track, at the precise instant he raises his foot to step forward.

To confuse your opponent, vary the length of your steps and your speed, but use short steps when changing position. You can only refine your sense of distance by moving smoothly and quickly.

While sparring or fighting, use good footwork to be as near to your opponent as possible for retaliation. Move lightly, with your knees slightly bent, always ready to spring forward when the opportunity arises.

Stepping forward with a feint adds speed to the attack and many times creates openings, as the opponent is forced to commit himself. Stepping back can be strategically used against an opponent who doesn't want to engage in close-quarter fighting—staying too far away to be reached.

In photo 1 , Lee remains at a far distance, cautiously waiting for the opponent to make his move. Just as his opponent launches his attack, in photo 2 , Lee quickly counters by moving in and clashing his leg to the opponent's lead leg, preventing him from delivering his high hook kick, as in photo 3. After stopping the attack, Lee takes the offensive by throwing a right punch, as in photo 4.

In order to beat his opponent to the blow, Lee needs quick reactions which came ·from his daily workouts, especially in developing his keen sense of awareness. You should also notice that he doesn't deliver his punch while his right foot is off the ground or when his body is not in alignment. His punch will make its contact as his body moves forward and his foot is just about planted.

You should always conceal your intention from your opponent.

Sometimes instead of countering by moving in, you do the opposite by moving back. In photos 1 and 2, Lee moves back and calculates the opponent's timing and attack. He moves just far enough to ward off the penetrating side kick, as in photo 3, and still be in a good position to retaliate, as he does in photos 4 and 5, with a punishing, punching attack.

In another illustration of the moving-back maneuver, the opponent fakes a punch to Lee's face, in photos A and B. Lee reacts to the feint, as in photo C, but is fast enough to recover and moves away from the real attack, as in photo D. He moves just enough to brush off the side kick and then counters—this time with a high hook kick to the opponent's face, as in photo E.

By retreating you allow the opponent some room to kick, so it is smart tactics sometimes to crowd or press him from launching his attack. A wise fighter strives to be an elusive and difficult

target by not moving forward or backward in a straight direction generally from a medium distance.

In both counters, Lee has to lunge forward to reach the opponent and has to do it quickly before the opponent can recover to defend himself.

Sidestepping

In jeet kune do, sidestepping is a defensive science to avoid a punch or a kick. If done properly, it is a safe and valuable movement for counterattacking. The criterion of sidestepping is not to avoid the opponent's onrush but his blow.

If the attack is shallow, the counter is quite simple. But if the attack is penetrating, such as a rush or deep lunge, it is not that easy. You have to move just enough to avoid the blow and be close enough to turn quickly and pounce on him just as he or the blow bypasses you.

In far distance fighting, the defender usually has the advantage because he has enough time to prepare for the attack and has time to counter accordingly. In photo 1, Lee waits for his opponent to attack and once the attack is on its way, he sidesteps to his left at the last moment, as in photos 2 and 3, barely avoiding the side kick. It is such a subtle movement that it does not "telegraph" or unbalance his body.

Once a kick or punch is committed, the attacker cannot deviate his blow from its path and expect to land it effectively. If he is off his feet, as in photo 3, he has no way to alter his course.

In photo 4, the opponent lands just in front of Lee, perfect for a counterattack. In photos 5, 6 and 7, although Lee is in a good position to use a front kick to his opponent's groin, he throws a right punch and follows up by dragging him to the floor.

Against an opponent's right lead punch, sidestep to the left by swaying your body and ducking your head toward the left without loss of balance. As his punch passes over your head, pivot your body by throwing your hips into the opponent and simultaneously delivering a right to his body or jaw.

Ducking is dipping your body forward from the waist mostly to

A

let the blow pass over your head. Its primary function is to avoid blows and still be in range to counterattack.

This tactic must be employed with caution. If you duck from a feint, or duck too early, you leave yourself wide open for a punch or a kick. Your only defense is to weave and quickly escape from that position. While ducking, keep your eyes constantly on your opponent and not on the floor. In photos A and B, Lee practices the tactic by swinging the heavy bag.

Most of your sidestepping should be to the left against an

unorthodox or right-lead fighter, because after he misses, he is defenseless as you stand behind him (*to the right, if he is an orthodox fighter*).

But in JKD, sometimes you are compelled to sidestep to the right to confuse the opponent. Sidestepping to the right requires more skill in timing and in countering. Your timing and movement must be better calculated than sidestepping to the left. You also have to counter faster because the opponent still faces you and is in position to deliver another attack.

In photos 1, 2 and 3, Lee avoids the side kick by sidestepping to his right. Notice that in photo 3, he uses his right hand to protect his body if he should ever misjudge the blow. In photos 4 and 5, Lee is in perfect position to deliver a kick to the groin area.

Frequently, your opponent is so intense in launching his attack that he is not prepared to protect himself after a miss. Generally he is vulnerable to an attack to the head and body. In photos A, B and C, the opponent lunges at Lee with a side kick. Lee quickly sidesteps to his right at the last moment to avoid the kick. Then he counters, in photos D and E, by employing a high hook kick to the opponent's face.

Precision of movement is essential in your footwork. Especially in sidestepping to your right, you must move at the exact moment and let the blow just miss you. If you move too early, you will

give the attacker time to change his tactic. It is better to move late than too early, but not too late and be hit.

Precision in movement means to move with balance. After avoiding the blow, you must always be prepared to defend against another attack or be prepared to counter. Precision can only be achieved by hours of training.

While shifting your feet to secure the proper distance, often use broken rhythm to confuse your opponent as to your distance. Be in the on-guard position to move quickly and easily.

When practicing offensive and defensive skills, you should always practice by combining footwork with them. No matter how simple the hand or foot techniques are, you should synchronize them while advancing and retreating. Eventually this type of training will develop your natural perception of distance and an ability to move gracefully.

Chapter VII
Skill in Hand Techniques

SKILLED HANDS

The hands are vital in most fighting;
  they are the shield and sword of a gladiator.

The hands are used mostly for hitting;
  but they are also defensive tools of a warrior.

The hands are more agile than the feet;
  they can move more quickly in any direction.

One who's skilled with his hands will beat
  most fighters in a martial arts competition.

Just imagine if you had no hands,
  what would you do in a real fight?

Yet there are many who do have hands,
  but have never learned to use them right.

Skill in Hand Techniques

Skill in punching doesn't mean only delivery and hitting your target. Accuracy, speed and powerful punches are just part of the technique of punching. Other elements include the position of your body when the punch is delivered, the path of your punch moving forward as well as returning, the way your punch is thrown.

The most used and the most important punch in jeet kune do is the leading straight punch. It is a fast punch as it travels only a short distance; it is an accurate punch as it goes straight forward; it is thrown with a minimum effort and consequently does not disturb your balance.

The leading straight punch is launched from an on-guard

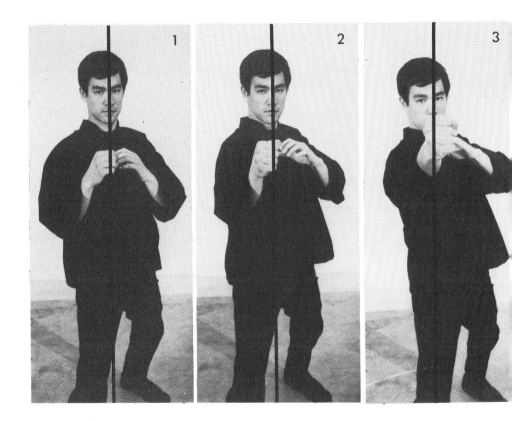

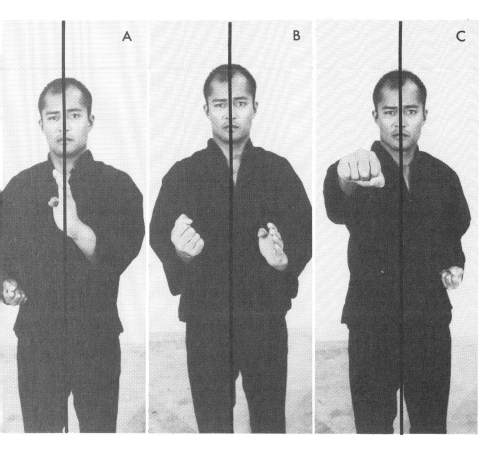

position and the trajectory of your punch should be a straight line in front of your nose, as in photos 1, 2 and 3—using your nose as the guiding point.

One of the big advantages of the JKD delivery is that you can throw a leading straight punch and still be well covered. Your body is protected and you are also in position to recover quickly from a miss.

In comparison, the classical system initiates its punch from the hip and exposes that section to an attack, as in photos A, B and C. When the punch is completed, it ends at one side of the body and the other portion of the body, especially the face, is exposed when the hand is withdrawn to the hip, as in photo C.

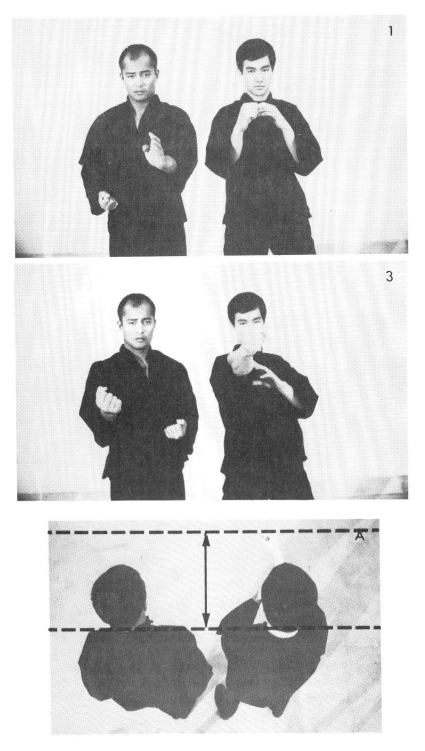

In the next series of photos, from 1 to 4, you will notice the difference in delivery between the JKD and the classical system. In the JKD system, as in photo 1, the hands protect the face and both the right and left sections of the body evenly. While in the classical, only the right side of the body is protected. In photos 2 and 3, the JKD fighter has already delivered his punch completely while the classical is still in the process. Photo 4 shows where the blow ends in both systems.

In photo A, Lee describes the short distance his punch has to travel over the classical stylist's from the on-guard position of jeet kune do. Apparently, this is why his punch reaches the target much more quickly, as you can see in photos 2 and 3.

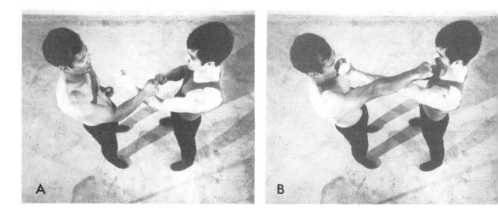

Throwing your punch with your fist kept vertically instead of horizontally like the classical, as in photo 1, affords you an extra reach, as in photos A and B. Lee's punch in this bird's-eye view, photo B, contacts his opponent but the opponent's punch, even fully extended, falls short.

The advantage of a JKD straight lead is that you can add three or more inches to your reach. In JKD both the straight short lead, as in photo X, and the long straight, as in Y, are used. The short is employed for close range fighting and the long for the middle distance. In photo X, Lee places his right hand on his left arm to indicate how much more extension he can administer in the long straight, as in photo Y.

The rear or "guarding" hand should always be held high to protect your upper body from a counterattack. The rear hand does most of the guarding and is a supplement to the other hand. If one hand is punching, the other should be returning to protect the body or immobilizing the opponent's arm or arms against countering. It should always be there, correlating to the uncovered line or unprotected area. And it should also be in a tactical position for a follow-up.

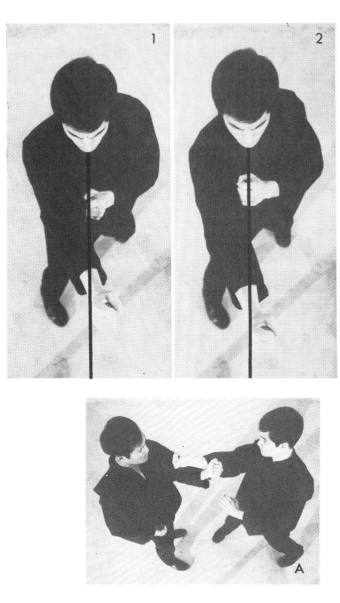

In photos 1, 2, 3, 4 and 5, Lee demonstrates from a bird's-eye view how he throws a combination of a lead right, follows up with a left and finishes off with a right. Notice the synchronizing of his hands as well as the protection they provide. Whether you punch with your lead or the rear hand, your punch should land at the same spot, using your nose as the guiding point.

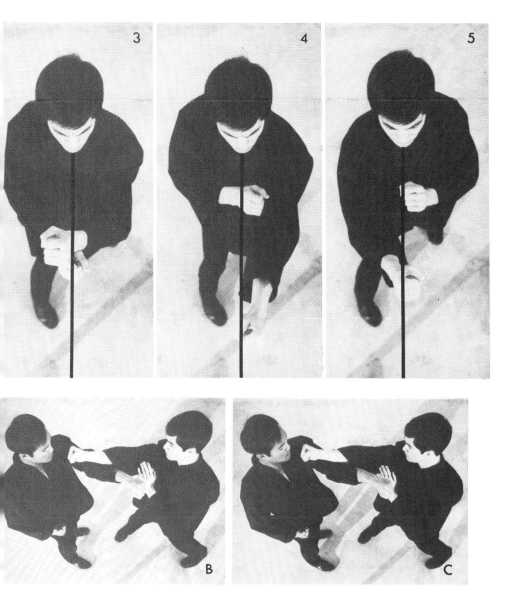

Punching straight before your nose and keeping your rear hand, is definitely superior to the classical, as Lee illustrates in photos A, B and C. As the lead hand is thrust forward, the rear hand is ever ready to block or parry any blow to the body. It is also ready to counter. In photo A, the punch is partially blocked but this doesn't stop it from penetrating and hitting the opponent's face.

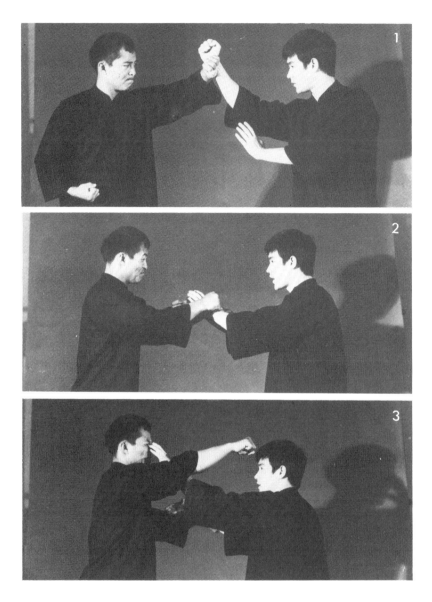

In this second illustration, in photos 1, 2 and 3, when Lee's lead punch is blocked, he throws a straight jab directly in front of his nose, which wards off the opponent's punch, as it proceeds straight toward his opponent's eye. Keeping the "centerline" thrust has a great advantage when two punches are thrown in the same path simultaneously against each other.

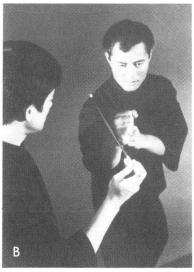

The position of your lead hand should allow you easy delivery and at the same time maximum security. In photos A and B (bird's-eye view), the hand is placed to deflect the blows to the side, and in photo Y, the punch is diverted downward with the defender hardly altering his hand.

As you have learned in chi-sao, your elbow must maintain

sturdiness, otherwise your defense may wither. Your elbow can move from side to side but must not collapse toward your body from a blow. After shooting out a punch, do not drop your hand when withdrawing it to the on-guard position. The punch should always be returned on the same plane or path it was delivered, as in photos 1, 2 and 3, ready for any counter.

Although you often see a good fighter with a bad habit, he usually gets away with it because of his superior speed and his good judgment in timing and distance. In photos A, B and C, Lee snaps back from a straight punch and counters with his left as the opponent creates an opening for Lee when he drops his hand in the withdrawal.

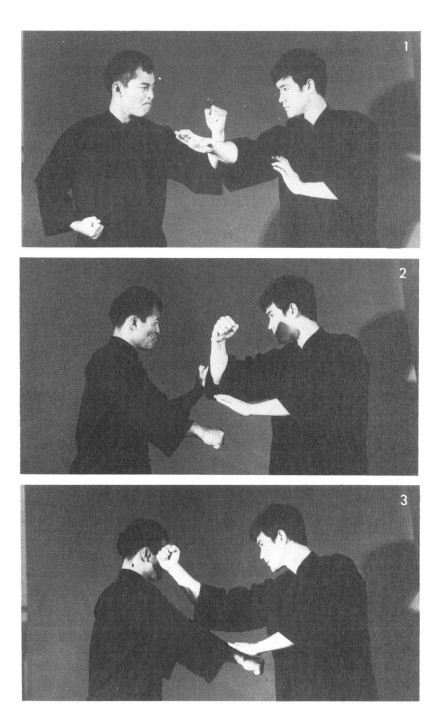

X

Y

In another illustration Lee converts a block by his opponent into a back fist punch when the opponent retracts his hand to throw another punch, as in photos 1, 2 and 3. If the opponent had left his hand, immobilizing Lee's right hand, in photo 1, and proceeded to punch with the other hand, he would have kept Lee on the defensive with his body punch. But the classical way of withdrawing his hand to his hip, has given Lee the chance to convert a block into an offensive weapon, as in photo 2. The opponent's second punch is easily stopped by Lee's rear hand, in photo 3.

Another bad habit some fighters develop is dropping their rear hand in the midst of exchanging blows, as in photos X and Y. In photo X, Lee takes advantage of such an opponent by slipping a punch and countering with a finger jab to his throat.

You can also take advantage of an opponent who lacks quick decision. He intends to throw his lead punch but after extending it halfway, he withdraws his hand to the on-guard position. During his indecisive moment, you can take advantage of his action by shooting a straight thrust, especially if he has already taken a step forward.

Z

Y

A

Then there is the fighter who continually engages and then disengages haphazardly. He will engage or contact your hand and instead of placing it there, lower or drift it to the opposite line, creating an opening for a quick, straight thrust.

In heavy punching, your arm becomes a weapon with your wrist, like a club, one solid piece. The forearm is the handle and the fist is the knot, as in photo A. The fist is aligned to the forearm with no bending of the wrist. At the completion of the punch your clenched thumb should be up. Your fist propels without a twist and the knuckles point at the direction of your body movement.

When punching with the lead hand, constantly vary the position of your head to protect it from a counter. Keep your opponent guessing. In your forward movement, during the first few inches your head remains straight, but later your head alters according to the situation.

Another tactic is to feint before leading to lessen any countering blow. But keep everything simple, do not overplay the feinting or head motion. Frequently, you can surprise your opponent with a double lead because the second punch may disrupt his timing and lead the way for a follow-up.

Sometimes a fighter attempts to put too much weight or "body" into his punch and consequently the blow becomes a push-punch—it lacks a powerful impact force. To be effective, the punch should always be delivered with your arms and shoulders loose. Your fist only tightens immediately before impact. Punches should never be thrown from a windup motion.

Some fighters have a good stance but as soon as they are ready to attack, they leave themselves wide open, as in Y. They develop this bad habit with bad training attitude, as in photo Z. When practicing with the heavy bag, always maintain good form, as in photo 1. Have your partner pay close attention to your faults.

Some martial artists practice their art in slow motion. They move their hands and feet as fast as the movement of a snail. But they claim that when the time comes, they can ward off any attack quickly and effectively even without speed training.

Bruce Lee used to emphasize that to be fast you have to practice fast movements. "I don't know of any sprinter in the world who can break the record only by jogging daily around the track," he said.

Muscles do not act by themselves without guidance. It is the nervous system which guides them to perform. A well-executed movement is the consequence of daily training for skill, by developing proper coordination of the nervous system with the muscles. These muscles contract at the exact fraction of a second with the precise degree of intensity or looseness, depending upon the command of the nervous system.

The coordination or connection between the nervous system and the muscles improves with each performance. Each effort not only strengthens the skill but paves the way for the succeeding acts to be easier, more definite and more exact. But absence from performance deteriorates the connection and affects the execution of the movement.

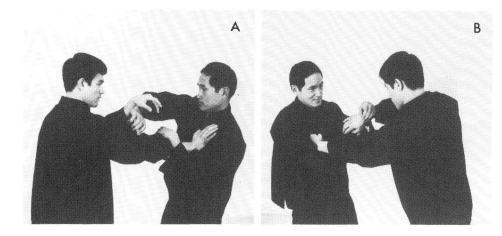

From the chi-sao (sticky fingers) exercise, as in photos A and B, the practitioners of wing chun advance to trapping hand (phon-sao) or grabbing hand (lop-sao) techniques. In photo 1, as Lee rotates his hand routinely in chi-sao, he feels his partner's flowing energy is being disrupted and flowing sporadically. At that instant—when there is a gap—Lee makes his move by overlapping his left hand over both of the partner's hands, as in photo 2. Then, as soon as he immobilizes or traps (phon-sao) them, he throws a straight punch to his partner's face, as in photo 3.

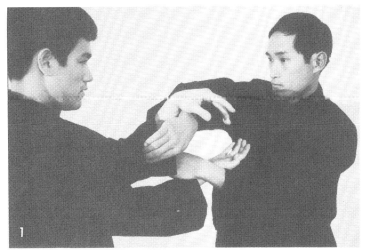

1

2

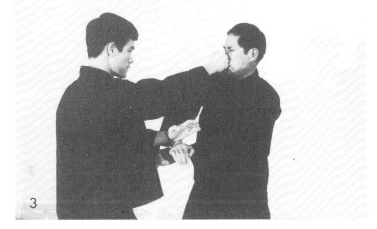

3

47

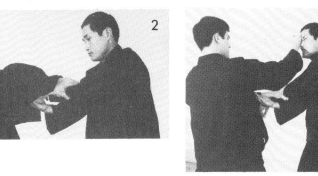

The chi-sao exercise is an important part of JKD borrowed from wing chun kung fu. First, it develops sensitivity and pliability in your hands, which are so valuable in close hand-to-hand combat. You can really frustrate your opponent who doesn't have that skill because every move can be easily thwarted once you have developed this sensitivity.

In photos 1, 2 and 3, Lee demonstrates the technique of grabbing (lop-sao) from the chi-sao exercise. In photo 1, Lee purposely exaggerates his rotation to narrow the space between his hands. When his hands are at the nearest position to each other, he grabs his partner's left arm with his left hand. During that instant, his arms cross each other, as in photo 2. Then Lee jerks his partner's arm toward himself and simultaneously delivers a back-fist punch to his face, as in photo 3. To learn more on the technique of grabbing and trapping, read *Wing Chun Kung-fu* by J. Yimm Lee.

From the close-quarters fighting, the students are taught to move further apart and continue to apply the hand techniques. In photos A, B and C, Lee's opponent attempts a finger jab utilizing the "centerline" thrust. He first attempts to push Lee's hand aside to create an opening, as in photo A. Second, he tries to penetrate Lee's defense with a finger jab but Lee's flowing energy is too powerful to oppose, as in photo B. In photo C, the situation completely turns around as Lee takes the offensive.

Although Lee always takes the stance of JKD on-guard position,

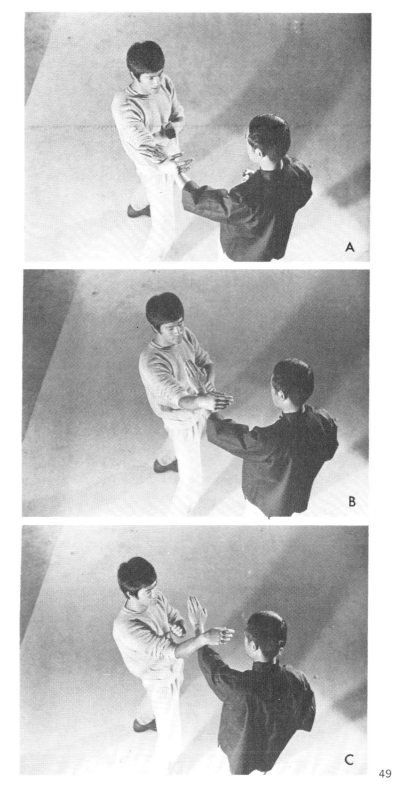

as in photo Y, for the sake of describing the evolution of wing chun techniques in JKD, he purposely stands in the modified wing chun stance, as in photo A, with his body leaning a little backward as he sinks his hips toward the floor. Unlike the wing chun stylist, who faces his opponent squarely, Lee adopts the right lead stance.

As the opponent drives his lead punch toward his face in photo

B, Lee with quick reaction and anticipation retaliates with a finger jab. By utilizing the centerline principle, Lee's thrust penetrates straight to the opponent's eye and simultaneously wards off his blow, as in photo C.

In the previous technique Lee's opponent fails to deliver the inner-gate punch but Lee's is successful. The reason is that this technique is not entirely dependent on execution but also on the intensity of your flowing energy.

In photos A, A1 and A2, the opponent engages Lee's right lead, but Lee quickly releases it with a small, counterclockwise motion, as in photo A1. Then he pivots his hips to his left as he simultaneously throws a right punch into his opponent's face, as in photo A2.

Against an opponent who hits and attempts to press his guard down, Lee uses the roll-and-trap maneuver, as in photos D to D2 (see page 52). In photo E, the opponent uses his forearm to hit and press Lee's right lead downward. Lee keeps his rear hand high for security and quickly rolls his arm to disengage, as in photo F. He continues to flow his energy and retain the immovable elbow position as he switches his weight to the front foot. Then he quickly traps the opponent's leading hand with his rear hand, as in photo D1. Once the opponent's hand is immobilized, as in photo D2, Lee quickly delivers a back-fist punch.

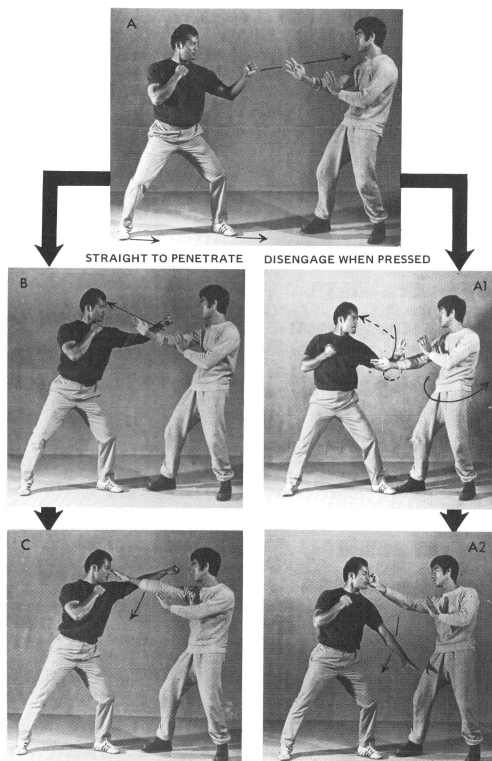

STRAIGHT TO PENETRATE   DISENGAGE WHEN PRESSED

ROLL TO DEFLECT   TRAP TO IMMOBILIZE

52

RECEIVES TO DETAIN   PURSUE WHEN WITHDRAWN

53

In photos G to G2 (see page 53), Lee illustrates a defensive maneuver of receiving a blow and then pursuing or countering when the hand is being withdrawn. For instance, when the opponent delivers a punch to his body, Lee steps back slightly and rides the opponent's punch with his lead hand, preventing him from penetrating, as in photos H and I.

When the opponent withdraws his hand to throw another punch, as in photo G1, Lee quickly counters with a jab, as in photo G2, using his rear hand to stop the second punch.

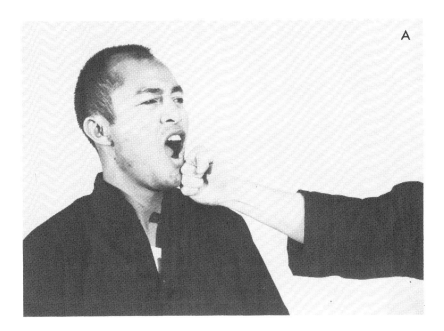

Blinking is a natural response of a man when an object is hurled toward his eyes. But in sparring or fighting, this reaction must be controlled or it will affect your defense as well as your counterattack. The instant your eyes are closed, you cannot react quickly enough to counter, as you may not know where your elusive opponent is. Second, your adversary can take advantage of your shortcoming by feinting an attack. He can fake a punch and as you blink, he can launch his blow while your eyes are shut.

While training in any type of fighting, it is important that you do not develop any bad habit that may cause injury to yourself.

One of the most common faults of a beginner is that he has a tendency to open his mouth while in the midst of exchanging blows. It is a habit he has acquired before studying martial arts, or he may have to breathe through his mouth because he is out of condition.

When your mouth is open, it can easily be broken by a direct hit, as in photo A. Another dangerous trait is to stick your tongue out, as in photo B. Learn to close your mouth in sparring or fighting by clenching your teeth firmly together. In sparring

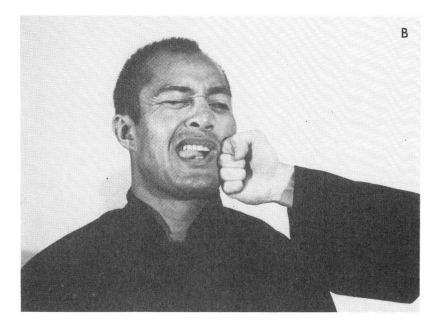

sessions, bite on your rubber mouthpiece to prevent it from flying out even after a hard contact.

Protect your hands and wrists by punching correctly. Punch with your fist by having your fingers tightly clenched, your thumb wrapped snugly over them so you can't break it. Since the knuckles are the hardest part of your fist, this is the section that should make the contact, not your fingers.

Prevent any chance of spraining your wrist by keeping it aligned and firm when punching. Learn to hit straight by practicing on a makiwara, canvas bag or the heavy bag.

Chapter VIII
Skill in Kicking

SKILL IN KICKING

The kick is used as the initial
  defense against an attack

Because it is the best arsenal
  launched from afar back.

The kick is a valuable asset
  against a skilled fighter,

Whose tactics you can't upset,
  and he knows when to counter.

Skill in kicking does come about
  when you practice real hard.

And this kind of drill you can tout
  as it will keep away the lard.

Skill in Kicking

Although the hands are considered the most important tools, the feet can be a vital and integral part in your overall strategy in fighting. For instance, against a clever boxer it is an advantage for you to use your feet all or most of the time. A boxer, who doesn't know any defense against a kick, is vulnerable especially at the low-line area around the groin and knee.

The strategy is to use your feet and stay away from his fists. This is possible because the leg is longer than the arm. Besides, a proper delivery of a kick is usually more powerful than a punch.

In jeet kune do the first line of attack or defense is the side kick to the shin or knee because that target is closest to you and it is exposed and difficult to protect. Furthermore, you are at a secure distance in delivering the kick which can cripple your adversary with one blow. Bruce Lee used to apply this low kick as a jab. His kick was so quick that he could deliver multiple blows in a second.

To do the low side kick, from an on-guard position, as in photo 1, slide your right or lead foot forward about three or four inches as you immediately bring your rear foot forward just behind the lead foot. Then simultaneously lift your lead foot, as in photo 2, and deliver a low side kick by thrusting your foot obliquely and twisting your hips strongly, as in photos 3 and 4. Learn to keep your body away from your opponent's reach by leaning away from him and not upright, as in photo A.

The leading side kick is the most powerful kick in JKD. One good kick is usually sufficient to knock your opponent off his feet. Although this is one of the favorite kicks, it should be employed with caution because it can be blocked or your leg seized if the kick is not delivered properly and at the right moment. But because of its tremendous force, sometimes it will penetrate a block or the block is not effective enough to keep the blow from scoring or maiming. The side kick is not fast nor as deceiving as some of the other kicks, but it can be used cleverly

when preceded by a feint. A good feint with your hands should open the defense for a quick side kick to the head or body.

The leading side kick can be used in a defensive tactic, also. For instance, as your opponent makes his move to attack, you "cut-off" or "stop-kick," intercepting his movement with a quick side kick to his body before his blow reaches you.

The best equipment on which to practice your side kick is the heavy 70-pound bag, as in photos A and B. The bag is durable enough to take any punishing blow and is heavy enough to give you a feeling of hitting a person. When contact is made, it emits a sound to let you know if the contact was solid or "pushy."

Sometimes it is a good idea just to keep side kicking the heavy bag as it sways back and forth. After a solid kick, wait for the bag to swing back, then time yourself with a leap and another side kick. Keep doing this for a good workout with your feet. Be careful that you don't miss the bag or fail to hit it squarely, because you are liable to hurt your knee after a strong thrust.

Another good drill is having someone stand behind the bag. After a solid side kick, instruct him to move a step back and hold the bag in a slanting position so you can deliver another kick without stopping your motion. To do the second kick, you must plant your foot down immediately after the initial kick and deliver another side kick without the three-inch slide. In other words, the second kick is like the first without the slide.

To do the high or medium-level side kick, stand at the on-guard

position. Slide your lead foot three or four inches, as in photo 1, then do the quick advance or the forward bust, as in photo 2, depending upon the space between you and the opponent. Just when your rear foot is being planted, your lead foot should be delivering the kick, as in photos 3 and 4. The power in the kick comes from a sudden twist of the hips before impact and the snapping of your foot after kicking through.

The side kick must be delivered with one fluid motion, as in photos A to D. From an on-guard position Lee fakes a punch to the opponent's face, as in photos A and B, luring the opponent to raise his hands, which leaves a gap in the midsection area. Then he quickly follows up with a side kick, as in photos C and D.

Other important apparatuses which Bruce Lee utilized constantly were the heavy shield and the air bag. The air bag is good as a stationary target, but the heavy shield is good for both stationary and moving targets.

Although the heavy shield cannot cushion the shock of the impact to the holder as can the air bag, the holder can nullify some of the shock by moving backward. Because the heavy shield allows mobility on the part of the holder, the kicker can unleash his most powerful kick without hurting the other person.

In photo 1, Lee prepares to attack from the on-guard position. The holder of the heavy shield begins to move backward as he sees the attack unfolding, as in photo 2. But he is not quick enough and Lee releases a side kick, as in photos 3 and 4. The kick almost drives the holder off his feet in photo 5. This type of training develops a sense of distance and improves the timing of both individuals. The air bag is not appropriate as a moving target because of its limited hitting space.

To kick high, have someone hold a long staff at your waist level. Stand about five feet away and raise your right foot as high as possible with your leg bent and slanted. This can be accomplished by lifting your knee as high as possible. Lean your body backward so your head inclines toward your right. Then skip on your left foot toward the staff until your right foot passes over it.

The purpose of this training is not to kick but to learn to lift your foot as high as possible. Keep increasing the height of the staff until your foot can't pass over it anymore. Then do the same exercise, minus the staff, and kick into the air. To kick much higher, for instance over your head, you have to concentrate heavily on flexibility types of exercises.

In your daily practice include the "rapid fire" side kick drill. Stand with your feet parallel, place your weight on your left foot, lean backward and execute a right side kick to your right. Then quickly position your right foot at the same spot after snapping it out. But just before you plant it, your left foot should be in motion for a left side kick to your left. As your left foot is being retrieved, immediately do another right side kick and keep repeating the kicks from one foot to the other as fast as you can. At the outset, you will feel awkward and off-balance but continue to practice this difficult exercise daily for several minutes until you can do it fluently and in balance.

One of the most utilized kicks in JKD is the hook kick. It is not a powerful kick but it is swift and deceptive. It is not a forceful kick but it can be damaging. The big advantage it has over the side kick is that it can be launched in many instances before your opponent can prepare for it. It is also a safer kick because you can

1

2

3

4

5

65

recover quickly after delivery. It is employed at a closer distance than the side kick but employed at a farther distance than in hand-to-hand fighting.

To do the hook kick, slide your lead foot three or four inches forward from an on-guard position, as in photo 1. Then do the forward shuffle or the quick advance. As soon as your rear foot is about to land, deliver your side kick, as in photo 2. The kick should be concluded with a snap and your body should be leaning back as in photos 3 and 4, and not forward.

Although the hook kick is used mostly for the upper line—above the waist—sometimes it can be used to attack the thigh or groin area, as in photo A. But this depends on the position of your opponent in relation to yours. He should be standing extremely to your right if you're at a right stance to hit his groin area. The hook kick to the thigh area is hardly ever used because it isn't too effective. The distance your foot has to travel is too short to generate enough power.

The spin kick is used mostly as a counterattacking maneuver. It is very effective against an aggressive opponent who keeps attacking in a straight line but not lunging at you. It is dangerous

A

2

1

to use this kick against a defensive or counterattacking opponent who constantly waits for your move before retaliating. Against such an opponent, you are vulnerable when your back is turned to him, just before you can shoot out your kick.

The spin kick is a little more difficult to execute because you must rotate your body, and in the process your back will be facing the target for an instant. At that point you can easily misjudge the position of the target. Frankly, it takes several hours of practice before you can even hit the target squarely.

The kick is not a sweeping kick as used by some martial artists but similar to a back thrust kick. This is one of the few kick techniques in JKD that employ the left foot.

The best equipment for practicing the spin kick is the heavy bag. Stand about a leg-length from the bag in an on-guard position, as in photo 1. Concentrate on the spot on the bag you wish to hit,

so that while your body is rotating like a swivel, as in photo 2, you can still picture the spot in your mind.

The pivot should be done on the ball of your right foot with your head slightly ahead of your lower body so you have a glimpse of the target before you thrust your foot out, as in photo 3. Your body should be aligned to the bag when you deliver the kick. Like the side kick you should "whip" your hips in at the time of contact and snap your foot, as in photo 4. It is very difficult to maintain your balance after the kick because your body is rotating and you must thrust your foot at the same time.

The spin kick is a surprise countering tactic. Even against a veteran fighter who has a good defense, the spin kick is often the only kick that can catch him off his guard. Because it takes so much practice to perfect this kick, learn to kick into the air as often as you can.

In the beginning, learn to do the technique slowly by standing at the on-guard position, as in photo 1, then rotate your body on the ball of your slightly bent foot, as in photo 2. Keep your other leg bent and ready to thrust. Be sure that the lifted foot does not swing haphazardly in the pivot or it will throw you out of balance. Besides, you can't kick effectively with an outstretched foot. Finally, thrust your foot with force when your body has made almost a complete 180-degree rotation, as in 3 and 3A.

The sweep or the reverse hook kick is not often used in JKD because it lacks power. It is used strictly as a high kick to the face. The kick is employed mostly as a surprise tactic, especially against someone who attacks with his leading foot extended. A front or hook kick will not work because the path of your foot will be hampered by the extended foot. But a sweep will work easily as it will avoid the obstructive foot.

To do the sweep kick, you have to have flexible legs. From the

3

on-guard position, as in photo 1, slide your lead foot about three or four inches forward and then do the quick advance as you initiate your kick, as in photo 2. If you are in the right lead stance, your foot will travel from your left to your right (clockwise motion) in a narrow arc, as in photos 3 and 3A.

This kick is a scraping type of kick and will not knock your opponent down. If done with your shoes on, it can cause damage by abrading your opponent's face.

To practice this kick on a heavy bag from a right lead position, stand slightly toward your left and hit the bag with one motion. The path of the foot should be almost vertical except for a small arc at the peak. The point of contact is the heel and outside blade of your right foot.

The latest kick that Bruce Lee developed for JKD was the inside kick. This kick is applied at the low line, especially to the groin and inside thigh areas. The point of contact is your instep.

The kick, which is as fast as the front and hook kicks, is used against someone whose stance is the opposite of yours. For instance, if you are in the right lead stance and your opponent is

in the left lead stance, you cannot hit his groin area with most kicks because his left leg protects it. But an inside kick which is delivered like a front kick, except it is not delivered vertically, can reach that area if you are standing slightly toward your left, angular to your opponent.

Unlike a front kick, the inside kick is delivered in an upward slant, opposite of the hook kick. But like the front kick, power can be created by jerking your hips forward just before contact. It is a difficult kick with which to generate power because you must have perfect synchronization between the hips and delivery of the kick.

The only other kick that is sometimes used is the front kick, which was discussed in the chapters on power training and speed training.

Chapter IX
Parrying

PARRYING

Parrying is a defensive tactic
that is easy to apply.

It is just a slap to divert
an oncoming blow.

Parrying can be automatic
if you train to comply.

It is an easy maneuver
once you know

That parrying is not the
same as blocking,

Which is much more forceful
and uncontrolling

'Cause it can tilt your balance
and stop your countering.

PARRYING

Parrying is a defensive tactic which can easily be learned and applied. It is a quick motion of your closed or open hand, either from the inside or the outside, to ward off blows directed at you. It is just a light slap to the opponent's hand with hardly any force, just enough to deflect the blow away from your body.

The technique should be done with your elbow almost at a fixed position and the movement coming from your hand and arm. It should not be an extreme reaction such as a slashing or whipping motion. Any excessive movement of your hand will expose your body to a counterattack. In other words, you should move your hand just enough to protect and control the blow.

Timing in this technique is more important than force. If you react too early, your opponent can either change the path of his kick or punch or you may leave openings for a counter. Parry late, waiting until the last moment and only acting when the blow is near to you.

Against a quick, penetrating opponent or against someone with superior height and reach, you may have to take a step backward while parrying. The parry should be made simultaneously with your back foot in motion and not after it is planted, nor should the parry be made prior to your body movement.

Learn to parry only against a real attack. But if you intuitively start to parry against a feint or false attack, your motion should be controlled so your hand or arm hardly react.

Train yourself to detect a real and a false attack by having someone direct various kicks and punches at you. After a considerable amount of practice, you will only parry at the real attacks and not react to the feints or fakes.

Generally, a parry is a good and safe defensive measure but a skilled fighter may beat your parry. If he does, then you have to move backward while parrying.

The inside high parry is generally utilized because most attacks are punches directed to the face. In comparing the classical style with JKD, as in photo A, it is discernible that the JKD way of parrying provides more protection and more speed on the upper line. Photo B reveals that a punch can be delivered almost simultaneously with the parry in JKD, but this is not true with the other style which uses a block and a punch—definitely a slower countering because of its two distinct motions.

Lee uses a long staff to practice the inside high parry, as in photos A and B. A partner thrusts the staff directly to Lee's face. Lee slips the thrust by shifting his weight to the lead foot and bending the front knee slightly. At the same time he uses his left hand to parry the staff lightly. This type of training is valuable because your partner can spot any discrepancy in your balance and motion. Against any heavy blow such as a kick, use your parry with clenched fist, as in photo 1.

To defend against a swing, Lee standing in the on-guard position, as in photo 1, prepares for the attack. As soon as his opponent initiates his swing, Lee already has his right hand in motion, as in photo 2. By the time he parries the punch, Lee's right punch is upon the opponent's face, as in photo 3. In photo Z, he uses the same parry against a straight right punch.

Z

The inside high parry is done with a slight, counterclockwise twist of your wrist as your hand meets the blow. This slight motion is capable of protecting your body because the twist of your wrist is away from your body and toward the oncoming blow. Your arm is stronger when it is directed away from your body rather than toward it. The classical uses the opposite motion. The twist is clockwise or toward the body.

A

The inside low parry is used against a punch or kick in the low-line area. From a right-lead on-guard position, the parry is made with a semicircular, clockwise, downward motion, as in photo 1. Simultaneously, your weight is shifted to the front leg as you bend your knee slightly. Almost at the same time, you counter with your right hand, as in photo 2.

In the classical system, your blocking hand moves downward in an oblique direction, as in photo A, as your other hand retracts toward your hip, as in photo 2. The disadvantage in the classical is that your countering is much slower since you have to block while retracting your other hand and then deliver your punch—two definite motions, while there is just one fluid motion of both hands in JKD. Another disadvantage is that your body, especially the upper line, is continuously exposed.

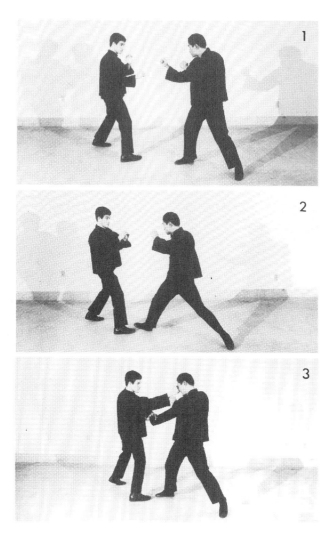

In the following photos, Lee illustrates the application of the inside low parry. In photo 1, Lee stands in the on-guard position, keeping his eyes glued on the opponent. As soon as the opponent begins to attack, Lee already responds to his action, as in photo 2.

The opponent throws a right that is intercepted by Lee's inside low parry, as in photo 3. Lee then converts the parry to a lop-sao or grabbing technique. In almost one smooth motion he pulls his opponent toward him and shifts his body forward to deliver a straight lead to the face.

The outside high parry is more a slapping stroke than the inside high parry, which is more a warding-off motion. This parry is to divert the blow on the opposite side of your body, so your hand has to cross over, as in photo A. There is no loss in quickness of counterpunching because your lead hand can still deliver the punch almost at the same time you are parrying. By utilizing the guard or rear hand for parrying, the lead hand, which is closer to your opponent and which is the stronger hand, is free to punch, as in photo B.

The classical system uses the same block for both the outside and inside high attack by just reversing the function of the hands. Instead of the left doing the block, the right does the blocking and the left or the weaker hand does the punching, as in photo Y.

Bruce Lee explains in the following series of photos how he utilizes his outside high parry for defense against a "head" shot. In photo 1, Lee waits for his opponent's first move. Then in the next photo, 2, as the opponent throws a right, Lee parries the blow with a light slap, just enough to divert the path of the blow from his face. Simultaneously, he takes a three or four-inch slide forward with his lead foot, bending his knee so the weight is placed on it.

Trapping the opponent's parried hand, he delivers his own right, as in photos 3 and 3A (side view). If Lee were to block or slap the blow vigorously, he would not be able to trap the opponent's hand to his shoulder.

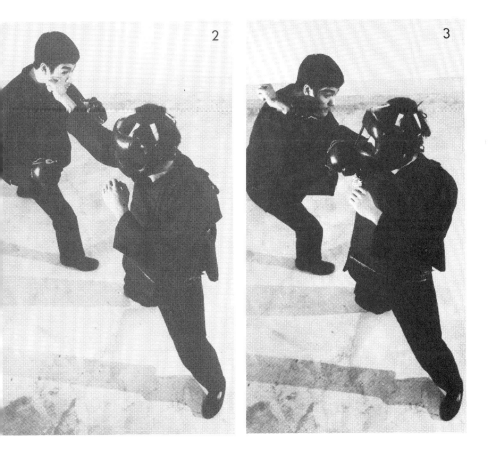

In the next illustration, Lee stands in the on-guard position preparing for the attack, as in photo 1. As the opponent initiates the attack, as in photo 2, Lee meets the left swing with a parry and counters by clawing the opponent's face, as in photo 3. Lee must time his forward movement and parry correctly to protect himself. In photo 4, Lee switches his hands smoothly so he has time to deliver another blow, this time a back-fist punch.

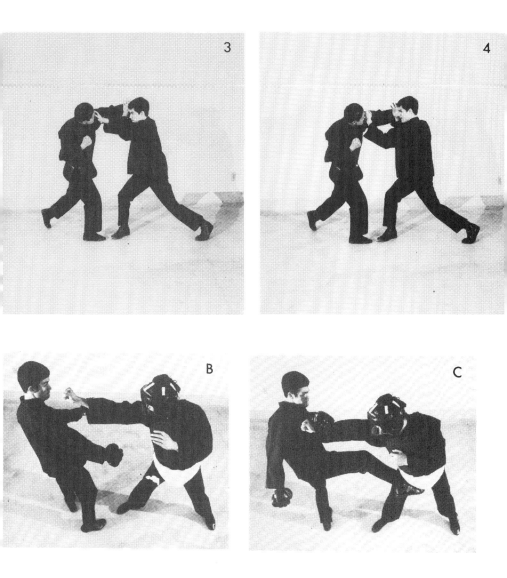

In this last illustration of the outside high parry, Lee uses the parry with a countering front kick. From an on-guard position, as in photos A and B, Lee parries a straight right. Without taking any step, he delivers a front kick to the opponent's groin almost at the same time, as in photo C. This is a safer parry than the preceding illustrations because he doesn't have to move in to reach his opponent, since the leg is much longer than the arm.

When Lee can't find a partner, he practices alone on the wooden dummy. In the next three photos, Lee practices his parrying technique. In photo 1, he parries with his left hand and uses his right for countering. In photo 2, Lee's parrying hand crosses underneath his punching hand. And in the next photo, 3, Lee parries with his left and simultaneously lets go a front kick.

The outside low parry against punches is performed almost similarly to the inside low parry except that in the former, the hand crosses over the body. The guard hand is used to protect the other side of the body against any low blow, as in photo A. Hence, the outside low parry has a greater circular motion than the inside low parry. Just like the inside low parry, its purpose is to deflect the oncoming blow downward.

The classical system uses the same blocking technique for all low-line blows. The hands just reverse their roles, as in B. The right hand is now used for blocking and the left is used for attacking. Like the other blocking techniques, there are two distinct motions instead of one fluid, continuous motion as in JKD.

In the next series of photographs, two classical fighters confront

each other as in photo 1. Standing in the orthodox stance, the fighter on the left throws a high punch which is blocked by his opponent, 2. Then the opponent follows up with a right punch but the fighter on the left blocks that, as in photo 3, and the fighter counters with a straight right to the opponent's solar plexus, as in photo 4.

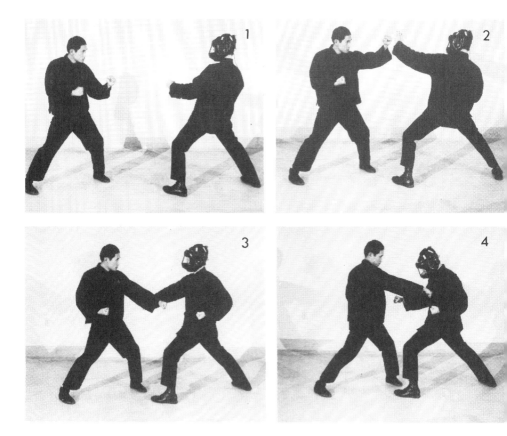

The same technique is now presented against an unorthodox (southpaw) opponent, using the JKD stance. Lee stands in the on-guard position, as in photo A, and as his opponent starts to attack, as in photo B, Lee sets to parry the blow, a slapping motion. Photo C shows the result of the parry and his countering to the face of the opponent.

A

B

C

91

Against an opponent who stands with his left lead (orthodox), as in photo A, Lee quickly stops the thrust by a short shuffle backward and parries it as the opponent steps forward with a straight right. Lee's parry here converts to trapping the opponent's hand just before he counters with a right to the face, as in photo B.

The outside low parry is usually used against a kick that is directed below your chest, with either a closed fist or an open hand.

The JKD and the classical parries seem similar in photos X and Y, but they differ in delivery. The parry in JKD is executed with a semicircular downward motion, just to deflect or control a kick. In the classical, the block is performed with a downward, slanting, forceful motion to stop the kick in its path.

In the next series of photos, Lee describes how he defends

against a lunging side kick. From the on-guard position Lee readies for an attack in photo 1. As the opponent lunges forward to launch his kick, Lee synchronizes his backward movement with the opponent's, as in photo 2. He also retreats just far enough to

avoid the blow but stays close enough to ward off the kick, as in photo 3. Lee takes advantage of the situation by turning his opponent completely around so his back faces him. Lee then quickly employs a front kick to the groin, as in photo 4.

Against someone who is in a stance opposite of Lee's, as in photo 1, Lee moves backward with perfect timing to the attack. Lee has more time in this attack as his opponent uses his rear foot, the farthest foot, to deliver a front kick. Lee just moves a little backward in this attack as the penetration is not that deep, in photo 2.

Lee parries the kick and prepares to defend against the next blow, photo 3. This time he uses the inside low parry against the right punch, trapping his opponent's hand. Then he counters with his own straight right punch, as in photo 4.

Lee constructed his wooden dummy with an extra arm in the center of the structure strictly to practice his low-line parry, as in photo A.

To parry is merely to close the line or deflect the opponent's hand; it should not swing too far to the right or left, just enough to create advantageous openings necessary to counterfighting.

Vary your parries to confuse the opponent. Don't let him set an attacking plan; instead keep him guessing. This will create hesitation on his part in launching his offensive maneuvers.

When there are a multitude of parries to be made, each parry must be completed and your hand should be at the appropriate position before the next parry is made.

When there is a compound attack, the first parry is performed with your movement of the rear foot and the second would be done exactly the same, as you are shuffling backward from the second attack. Your rear foot must move before the attack and not after the delivery of the blow.

Parrying is more subtle than blocking, which is a more violent force as it is used frequently to abuse the opponent's limbs. Blocking should be used infrequently and only when necessary, because it can drain your energy. Besides, even if you block a well-delivered blow, it will still disturb your balance and create openings for your opponent. In the meantime, it prevents you from countering.

Chapter X
Targets

TARGETS

You can't be a nice guy in a fight
  because it may be your life.

Kicking the groin is all right,
  even jabbing the eyes like a knife.

Fighting is not just hitting
  but aiming at the weak spots of your foe.

End it with a single belting,
  instead of using more than one blow.

There are several targets on a body
  vulnerable to a smite.

But you must be proficient and ready
  to hit with all your might.

TARGETS

The two primary targets in fighting are the eyes and the groin, as in photo A. A solid groin blow can quickly incapacitate or even cause death to a man, no matter how powerful he is physically. Even a light blow can render a man unconscious.

In some martial arts they will call such a vicious blow too cruel and inhumane. But Bruce Lee always felt that your main purpose in learning the martial arts or self-defense arts is self-protection or self-preservation.

PRIMARY TARGETS

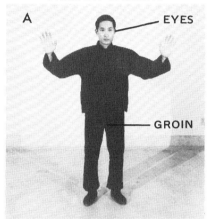

"The meaning of 'martial' is 'warlike,' " he used to say. "We are not in a game; it's your life or his. And since you only have one life, take care of it the best you can.

"When you treat the martial arts like a sport," he said, "then you have established rules which create weaknesses. Or when you attempt to be too civil, then you learn to resist for fear of hurting your adversary and this can also weaken your defensive technique."

Many fighting arts, which became sports, establish rules that forbid certain, dangerous techniques to the players. Consequently, most rules banned attacking the groin area and as time went by, emphasis on guarding the groin area lessened to almost nothing. This is true in boxing, wrestling, judo and many styles of karate. Because of the artificial protection today, many fighters do not know how to protect themselves from a kick to the groin, as in photo X. Even their stances are vulnerable to a fast, frontal kick.

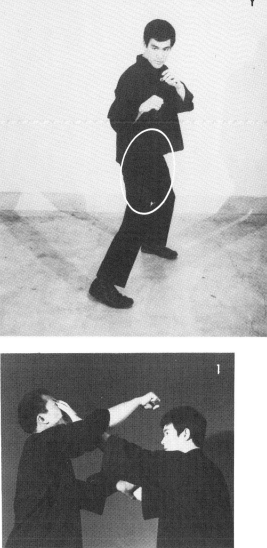

Lee saw this flaw and created his own stance, as in photo Y. In this stance, the groin area is well-protected by the lead thigh and by his adaptation of the shuffling footwork. It did not curtail his speed or freedom of footwork.

Another feature of JKD is that the rear foot is rarely used for kicking except in a spin kick. The reason for this is that when the rear foot crosses the front, at that moment your groin area is exposed, especially with a roundhouse kick.

Finger-jabbing to the eyes, as in photo 1, a primary target, is also considered the first line in hand technique for attacking and

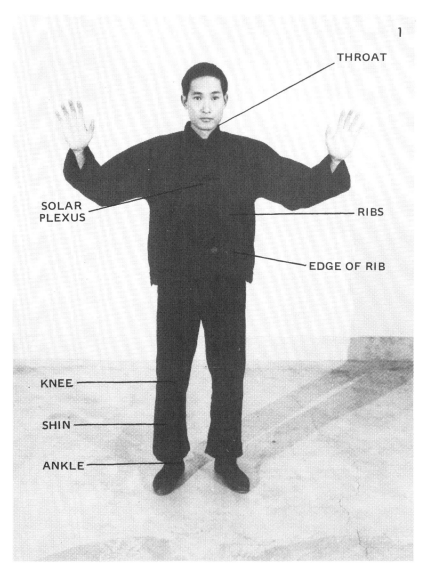

defending, while the shin or knee kick is the first line in kick technique. Eyes are a primary target because once blinded, one is almost helpless to defend himself. It is referred to as the first line of offense or defense because finger-jabbing allows you an additional three or four inches in reach over a punch.

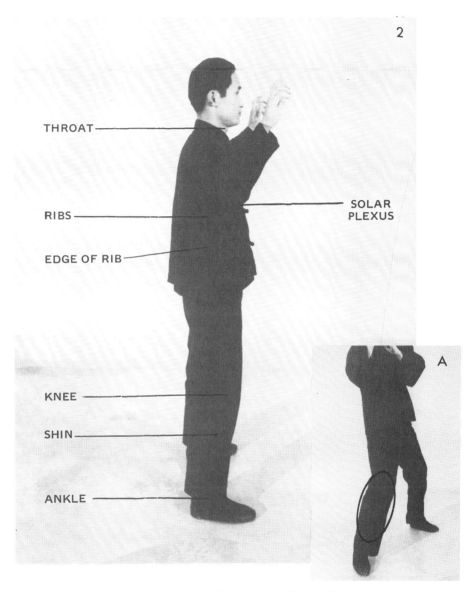

Besides the primary targets, there are other vital spots in a human body, as in photos 1 and 2 (side view). The knee or shin kick is the first line of attack or defense because the leg allows you the longest reach and the knee or shin generally are the targets closest to you, as in photo A.

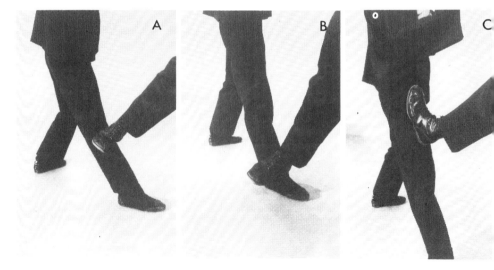

A   B   C

The blow to the lead leg can be a side kick to the knee or shin, as in photo A, a side kick to the ankle, as in photo B, or to the thigh, as in photo C. The kick to the lead leg is a fairly safe kick if delivered correctly, as in photo 1.

The upper-line areas are harder to hit because they are usually better and easier to guard. To hit the throat of a skilled fighter is almost impossible because his hands are always guarding it, and he tucks his chin to his shoulder, hardly allowing an opening. Sometimes a finger-jab can penetrate, as in photo Y.

The rib cage is very vulnerable, especially if a blow is administered when the hand is held high. In such a position, the ribs are separated considerably and as a result, are quite fragile to any kind of a sharp blow.

The solar plexus is one of the most vulnerable spots in your body but is hard to hit. It is a tiny spot to hit and most fighters have their hands there all the time. A good hit there usually discourages one from continuing to fight, but it is a rare occasion when a skilled fighter can be hit at that spot.

The jaw is a larger target than the throat but it is an elusive

Y

target against a skilled fighter who can weave and duck. A fighter with good footwork can move away or just move his head away from the blow. By tucking his chin to his shoulder and by raising his shoulder to meet it, it becomes an inaccessible target to hit. Nevertheless, a hit to the jaw can be devastating, as in photo Z. There are more boxers knocked out from a hit to the jaw than to any other place. Besides, if a blow is delivered at a certain angle, as in photo Y, the jaw can easily be broken.

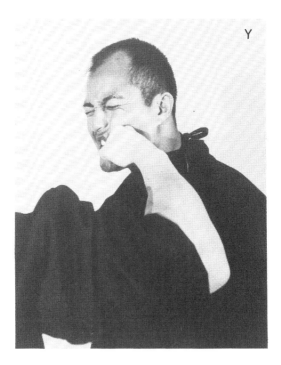

The science of fighting is not just to hit your opponent's body, but to hit him at the most vulnerable spot. Better to finish a fight with one punch than with several.

You also have to learn to hit without injuring yourself. Your fists must be formed properly or you can injure your thumb, fingers or your wrist. If you punch or kick correctly, you will not hurt yourself even if you miss your target and hit a harder substance.

In delivering a side kick, use the edge or flat of your foot to

contact the target as in photo A. Occasionally, you may be able to use your heel, as in photo B. If you are wearing shoes, the point of contact for a front kick can be the toe, as in photo C, the ball of your foot, as in photo D, or your instep, as in photo E. But if you are barefoot, avoid using your toes and use caution when using the ball of your foot. The safest is your instep. Sometimes the inside portion of your foot is employed, as in photo 1, but usually for sweeps.

The strategy of fighting depends upon the vulnerable spots that you must protect as well as the areas most easily within the reach of your opponent.

B

1

C

D

Chapter XI
Sparring

SPARRING

In sparring, you will learn to hit
with rhythm and perfect timing,

But many times you may want to quit,
when you're the one receiving

Blows to your head and your body
which sting and give you a headache.

Don't despair 'cause you're unwieldy;
keep on sparring 'til you can take
kicks and punches to your body.

Unless you spar, you'll never know
how you'll do in a real fight.

Like learning to swim, you must go
into the water to overcome fright.

SPARRING

Contact sparring is the closest endeavor to real fighting. Unlike real fighting, there are limitations such as wearing protective gear and gloves as well as restrictions in the use of certain offensive techniques. Until man invents better equipment and methods, this is the most practical way to train today.

Bruce Lee always emphasized the importance of sparring. "A fighter who trains without sparring is like a swimmer who hasn't immersed in the water," he used to say.

There are shortcomings in modern, fighting sports. In Western boxing the participants have the inclination to become reckless because of the protective rules in the sports. They are restrained from using certain punches, prohibited from hitting below the belt and they are not allowed to use their feet to kick.

Those who participate in the Oriental martial arts tournament, such as karate, are being over-protected by the noncontact practice of stopping the blows several inches from the body, even though the full body is the target. This practice hurts the participants' ability to judge distance. Besides, this artificial shelter contributes to the abstinence of learning to slip, duck, weave and the other defensive tactics used in boxing.

In real or total fighting, all the elements must be employed to be effective. You must use distance as a protective maneuver and all the evasive techniques of close fighting.

The science of fighting is the ability of one to outsmart and out-maneuver his opponent; to hit him without getting hit. In

A   B

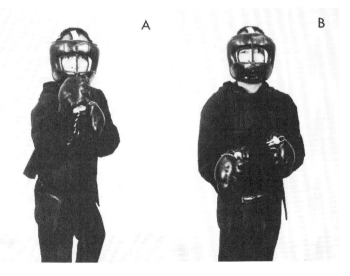

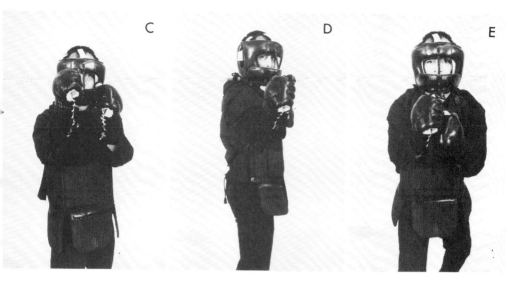

C D E

fighting, a good offense is the best defense, as in many other sports. A good fighter should beat his opponent to the punch with lightning-fast leads or out-kick him with his quick lead foot. He attacks with deception. He creates openings for himself by his command of techniques that lead his opponent into a quandary. He must deliver proper kicks and punches instinctively, so his mind is free for strategy.

Although sparring with a pair of gloves and other protective gear is cumbersome and weighty, it is the best way to gain some experience in simulated fighting conditions. The headgear will affect your vision and the gloves will be cumbersome and heavy, but you must continue to use good posture and technique. You must be careful not to fall into a habit of careless defense while wearing the protective gear.

Keep your hands at the proper position, as in photo A. They should not be too low, as in photo B, because this leaves openings to your face and upper parts of your body. By keeping your hands too high, as in photo C, the lower line areas are open and it also prevents you from delivering an effective straight, fast punch without first repositioning your hands. Besides, it also blocks out your vision. Standing too much to the side, as in photo D, prevents you from utilizing your rear hand for defense or offense. Being too square, as in photo E, hinders you from rapid forward or backward movement and also exposes your vulnerable groin area.

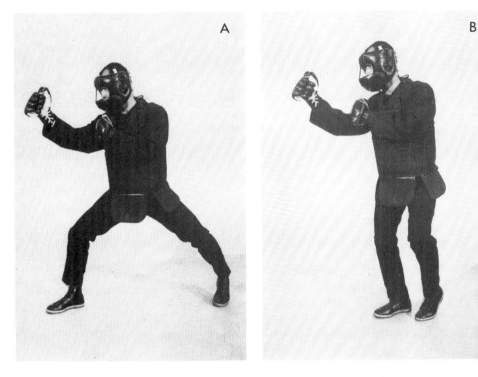

Punching from too wide a stance, as in photo A, weakens your blows because you cannot utilize the full rotation of your hip motion. You are also handicapped in penetrating or retreating quickly and your front foot becomes an easy target to your opponent.

Sparring with your feet too close, as in photo B, upsets your balance and prevents you from delivering a strong punch. Do not throw a punch while leaning back, as in photo C, because there is absolutely no power in such a punch. A punch must be thrown with your body upright and in balance, with the weight shifting to the lead foot. If you ever have to lean your body backward, reposition properly before delivering. Why throw a punch if it is not effective?

Another ineffective blow is hitting while backing away. Your weight has to be shifted forward to have force. In other words, step back, stop, then hit. After the punch, if you have to keep backing up, do the same routine: step back, stop, then hit.

It takes good sense of distance and ability to stop in your

retreat instantly and unexpectedly. Learn to maneuver quickly from defense to offense and vice-versa.

An easy habit to fall into is to punch with your body leaning too far forward, as in photo D. Throwing a punch in this awkward position is futile since you cannot exert enough power into the blow when you are out of balance.

Like a good Western boxer, a skilled fighter should be able to hit from any angle. Each punch prepares him to deliver the next. He is always in balance to shoot any kind of punch. The more skillful he becomes as he learns more effective combinations, the more different types of opponents he will conquer.

You have to learn to be patient while sparring. Don't deliver your blows until you are certain to hit your opponent. Step toward him when you punch to make contact. Hit as straight as possible, using your nose as the guide in the delivery. Don't overshoot your target because a miss leaves you out of position and a target for an easy counterpunch, especially against a boxer who leads. Instead, beat him with lightning-fast leads and draw his counterpunches with feints so he will miss.

Feinting is to deceive an opponent into reacting to the motion of your hands, legs, eyes and body. Your feint should entice him to adjust his defense, thereby creating momentary openings. Reaction to a slight wave of the hand, stamp of the foot, a sudden shout, etcetera, is normal human behavior. Even an athlete with years of experience will be distracted by such demonstration.

No feint is effective unless it compels the opponent to react to your wishes. To be successful, it must appear to be a simple movement of attack—the combination of hitting with the feints should appear to be the same.

A feint should be fast, expressive, threatening, changing and precise, followed by a clean, sharp blow. Feints are not as imperative against an unskilled fighter as against a skilled one. Between two evenly-matched fighters, the one who is the master of the feint will be the winner.

There are several methods in which to execute the feint. From the on-guard position move forward and without any hesitation bend your lead knee quickly. This slight motion creates an illusion that your arms are also moving when they aren't. Another feint is the false thrust. Move your body above the waist by simply bending your lead knee and extending your front hand slightly. Then as you advance, take a longer step with your front foot and do a half-extended arm thrust. The thrust must appear real to induce the opponent to parry. When the opponent parries, disengage your hand, and deliver the real thrust with either hand. If the opponent can be reached without a lunge, keep the arm slightly bent and keep yourself well protected by shifting, or by means of the rear guard. The arm should be more fully extended if the feinting precedes a kick or a lunging attack. Another successful feint is to bend your upper body only while advancing.

The one-two feint can be employed "inside-outside and outside-inside" or "high-low and low-high" with one or both hands in combination. The initial feint must be long and deep but quick, in order to draw the parry. The next response is to hit the opponent hard before he can recover. This feint is a "long-short" rhythm.

In the "long-short-short" rhythm or the two-feint attack, the first feint must force the opponent to the defense. At that moment, the distance is closer for a short feint before delivering a short but real hit.

The "short-long-short" rhythm is a more advanced form of feinting. The opponent is not induced by the first feint so the second feint is made long to mislead the opponent into thinking that it is the final thrust of a compound attack, thereby drawing him to parry. In this tactic, speed and penetration are the elements for success.

To prevent or lessen the chance of being countered heavily, leads should consistently be preceded by feints. But the continuous use of the same feint will defeat your purpose because the opponent can take advantage of this maneuver for a counter-attack. Combinations of feints must be practiced until they become automatic. You must also train in the use of various types of feints to learn the different reactions from your opponents.

The immediate advantage of a feint is that from the outset you can lunge to attack with a feint to gain distance. In other words you can shorten the distance with a lunge and gain some time from the false attack by causing the opponent to react or hesitate.

The feints will be more successful after several real but simple attacks. This will confuse the less mobile opponent who will not know if the attack is real or not. It may also excite a lightfooted opponent to flee. But if an opponent doesn't respond to your feint, attack with straight or simple movements.

There are several ways of feinting: (1) feint a jab to his face and hit him in the stomach; (2) feint a low sidekick to his shin and deliver a hookkick to his head; (3) feint a jab to his face and deliver a sidekick to his stomach, and (4) feint two jabs to his face then hit his stomach, etcetera. Experiment with other feints to create openings.

Drawing is almost like feinting. Actually, feinting is a segment of drawing. In feinting, you attempt to deceive your opponent to react to your motion. In drawing, you leave part of your body uncovered to lead the opponent to attack that area. As he does, you are prepared to take a defensive measure and are ready to counter.

Drawing is also a strategy to lead the opponent to respond to your deception and when he does, he is caught in a trap. For instance, you may retreat quickly to entice the opponent to lunge an attack. As he does, you are ready to evade the attack and counter with a specific blow.

Speed and timing complement each other. A fast blow will not be powerful unless thrown with timing. In photo A, a punch is thrown ineffectively because of poor sense of timing and distance.

You do not have to move with a rapid or jerky motion. Many times a smooth, unhesitant movement from rest and without apparent preparation will hit the target because it is so unpredictable.

Timing is the capability to perceive the right moment for action, such as when the opponent is preparing or planning to move; when the opponent is in the midst of a movement; when the opponent is at a tense disposition, or when the opponent's concentration is in the doldrums.

Timing in fighting means perfect delivery as the opponent steps forward or is drawn into stepping forward. If your timing is off and you launch your blow too early, as in photo X, your energy is spent without any telling effect. If your delivery is too early, as in photo Y, then your blow is not too effective, as your force was still developing.

Timing a blow is the secret of powerful blows but no one can be a really heavy hitter even with perfect timing unless he has complete confidence in his own ability. Timing can be a mental problem, especially when your rhythm is broken. Your mind has difficulty in adjusting to the sudden interruption of your movement while it continues for a fraction of a second. This

X

A

Y

"half-beat" is psychologically disturbing because you expect a full-count movement but your opponent attacks halfway before the count is completed.

Speed is not the chief prerequisite when two fighters of equal ability and speed are matched. There is a slight advantage to the first one who attacks but a greater advantage to the one who knows how to break the rhythm. Even with only moderate speed his half-beat or unexpected movement can catch his opponent flatfooted when his rhythm or cadence is interrupted and he can't adjust quickly enough.

Even with a pair of heavy gloves, you must continue to use basic training, such as nontelegraphing your blows. Your delivery will not be as efficient with those gloves on, but continue to practice this way as it will increase your proficiency in the technique—with or without gloves. Since your foot is not burdened with protective gear, kick naturally with speed and force in your sparring. Do not deliver a kick, as in photo 1, forewarning your opponent of your intention.

A

In boxing and in some Oriental martial arts, the hands are the primary and almost the only assets for offense and defense. But in other martial arts the kicks definitely play a heavy part in strategic fighting. Unfortunately, many schools emphasize the foot too heavily and ignore the hand technique.

Bruce Lee used to mention that the hands are the primary weapons for attacking and defending. The foot can be contained by placement of your foot to the opponent's, as in photo A, and by closing in on him. But the hands are much more difficult to contain because they can be thrown from close quarters and from all angles.

There are other techniques besides parrying to defend against punches. Often it is better to use an alternative method such as footwork, because you are usually in a better position to counter. Other alternatives are evasive tactics such as slipping, rolling, weaving and bobbing.

Slipping is evading a blow without moving out of countering range. Your timing and judgment must be perfect to be successful as the blow should miss by a fraction of an inch.

Although slipping can be executed either inside or outside a straight lead, the outside slip is preferred. It is safer to use and prevents the opponent from preparing for a counter. The idea is to turn your shoulder and body to the right or left so you can slip the blow over either one of your shoulders.

Slipping is a valuable technique in sparring because it allows you to use both hands for countering. And you can hit harder moving inside a punch than blocking or parrying and then countering.

The small rotation of your heel is frequently the answer to successful slipping. To slip a right lead over your left shoulder from a right lead stance, raise your rear heel and rotate it clockwise, transferring your weight to the lead foot. Simultaneously bend your lead knee and turn your shoulder in the same clockwise direction so you will be in a position to retaliate.

To slip a lead over your right shoulder, raise your lead heel and rotate it counterclockwise, transferring your weight to the back foot. Simultaneously, bend your rear knee and turn your shoulder in the same counterclockwise direction, preparing to counter with a right hook.

The science of bobbing and weaving is a valuable tactic to avoid blows and improve your defensive measures to counter with a more powerful punch such as the hook. It provides you with access to the use of both hands for attacking whenever an opening develops.

Weaving in sparring is to move your body from side-to-side and in-and-out. In the process you also keep slipping straight leads directed to your head. It makes an elusive target of your head as your opponent is uncertain which way you will slip. Also, he is in a dilemma because he doesn't know which hand will deliver the punch.

To weave to the inside against a right lead, slip to the outside position first by dropping your head and body with a turn of your shoulder and bending of your knee. Close in under the completed punch and quickly resume your stance. The opponent's hand should be over your left shoulder. Keep your hands high and near your body. Then without stopping your motion completely, swing your body to the inside position and engage your right hand to the opponent's left. Continue to weave and simultaneously counter with right and left punches.

To weave to the outside against a right lead, slip to the inside position by dropping your head and body with a twist of your upper body and bending of your knee. Then move your head and body in a circular, counterclockwise motion so that the opponent's right hand is over your right shoulder. Keep your hands high and near your body. You should be at the outside position by then, standing in the on-guard stance.

Weaving is more difficult than slipping, but you must master slipping to be skilled in weaving. The key to weaving is to learn the art of relaxation.

Weaving is seldom used by itself. Usually it is accompanied by bobbing. Bobbing in fighting is usually referred to as moving the head constantly vertically, rather than side-to-side. The way to bob is to barely sink under a swing or hook with a controlled motion. Your body should be in balance at all times, to counterattack or to slip straight punches even at the bottom of the bob. Don't counter or straight-down bob except to the groin. Keep your hands high and use your knees for motion.

The purpose of bobbing and weaving is to close in by sliding under the opponent's attack. Weave to employ belated counters of hard, straight punches or hooks. The master of bobbing and weaving is usually a hooking specialist, who is able to dominate taller opponents. Like other skills in fighting, your weaving and bobbing must not be too rhythmic. You must keep the opponent confused at all times.

Rolling is moving your body in such a manner that the blow is wasted. For instance, against a straight punch and uppercut, you move backward. Against a hook, you move to your left or right. You do the same against a hammer, except you also move downward in a curved motion.

Always use evasive tactics with countering kicks or punches. Keep your eyes wide open as blows do come without much warning, and utilize your elbows and forearms for guarding. Evasive tactics, when used with hard hitting, can discourage an aggressor and turn the scuffle into grappling. When evasive maneuvers are not used, parry blows that are directed to your head.

Skill in footwork can be developed greatly during sparring sessions, as your feet can move freely in any direction. Although circling, as in the evasive tactics, is not practiced too heavily in the Oriental martial arts, it is an important segment of close fighting when the use of kicks is not feasible.

In circling to your right, the lead foot is the axis to move your body to the right. The first step with your lead foot can be either long or short, depending on the situation. The shorter the step, the smaller the pivot. Keep your lead hand slightly higher than normal to prepare for a countering left punch.

Circling to the right is used to nullify a right lead hook, to keep the opponent off-balance and to deliver an advantageous left-hand counter. It is important to maintain your basic posture, move deliberately without any exaggerated motion and never cross your feet.

Circling to your left should be employed more frequently than the right because it is safer. You can stay out of range from rear, left-hand punches. But it is more difficult to do, as it requires shorter steps to be exact in your movement.

The step-in and step-out are offensive maneuvers to create openings and are often used with a feint. The initial movement is to step-in directly with your hands held high, creating an illusion of delivering a blow. Then you step-out quickly before your opponent can counter. The strategy is to induce him into complacency so you can deliver a surprise attack.

A fighter with fast footwork and a good lead can impress upon others that the art is simple and easy. He can make a slower opponent look bad by the process of hit and run. As the opponent moves in, he confronts him with a lead punch and quickly steps back. As the opponent pursues, he repeats the process—circling and moving in and out. Occasionally, he will meet his opponent head-on with a straight right or left or a combination.

Even while you are waiting in the on-guard position, your hands and body should be in continuous motion, slightly bobbing. The motion can deceive and camouflage your attack as well as keep your opponent confused. The motion should not be overdone or it will disturb your timing in attacking and defending.

In sparring, learn to be patient. Do not waste your energy by throwing a punch until you are almost certain that it will hit the target with power. Throwing a punch by over-reaching, as in photo

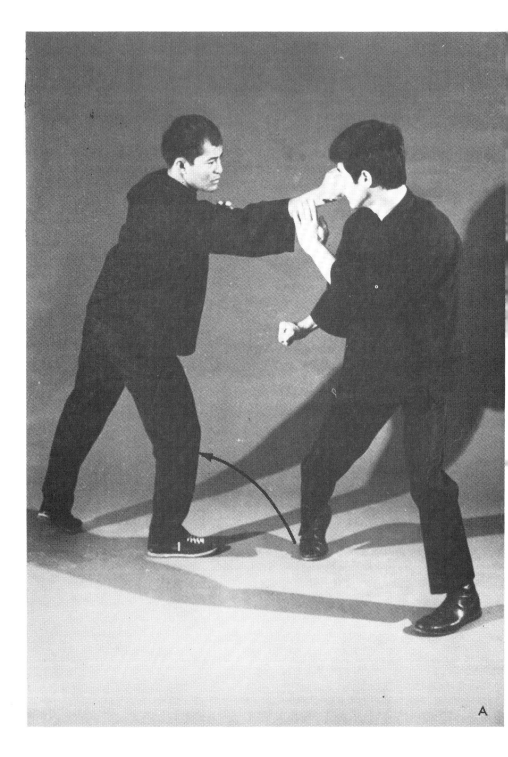

A

A, is risky. First, your punch is too weak to do any damage even if it makes contact. Second, you place yourself in a precarious position against a counterpunch. And third, you have not locked your foot to the opponent's, allowing him freedom to deliver a hook kick to your unprotected groin.

Back your opponent into a corner or to the ropes before you attack. Throw accurate punches as you have him cornered. Missing too many times can easily wear you down.

X

Z

For long-range sparring, jab with your lead, as in photo X, and cross with your rear. Judge your distance correctly before throwing a punch. For short range, use hooks, rear hand body blows and uppercuts, but do not punch from too far out, as in photo Z. Punch through your opponent.

Weave as you hit. A hard punch can only be delivered from a solid base. Occasionally take a short step to the left, three or four inches, with your rear foot when throwing a right lead punch. This will put more power in your punch, especially from long range.

Don't ever punch with your foot off the ground, as in photo A.

Have confidence when you spar. Don't move away from your opponent when you are delivering a punch, as in photo B. Your punch will lack power and you will also reveal to your opponent a fear of being hit. Your timid action only increases his confidence and decreases your chance of fighting with strategy. Another bad gesture is to turn your head away from the attack, as in photo X. Such behavior leaves you open for additional attacks and prevents you from countering.

A   B

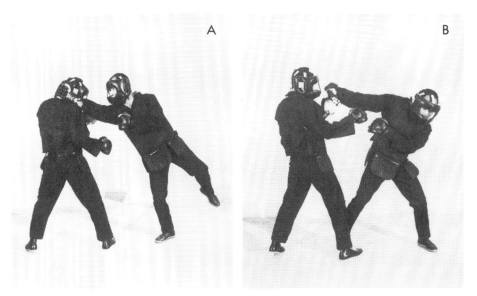

During sparring is the time to learn your weaknesses and how to overcome them. It is too late in a real fight. You will be surprised to learn your pitfalls while sparring. Bad habits, such as standing with your feet parallel, may show up. You may only notice it when you find yourself easily being thrown off-balance, as in photo Y.

You may be retreating with your guard down, as in photo Z. But you will learn quickly to keep your guard up after you take several hard blows to your face.

There are so many variables in fighting that you cannot follow through a stringent plan. You have to be flexible as different situations arise.

X

Y

Z

BRUCE LEE-1940-1973

Bruce Lee flashed brilliantly like a meteor through the world of martial arts and motion pictures. Then, on July 20, 1973, in Hong Kong, like a meteor—he vanished, extinguished by sudden death. He was just 32.

Bruce Lee began his martial arts studies with wing chun, under the tutelage of the late Yip Man, to alleviate the personal insecurity instilled by Hong Kong city life. Perhaps because his training enveloped him to the point of fanaticism, he was eventually able to refine, distill and mature into a philosopher, technician and innovator of the martial arts.

After intensive study of different martial arts styles and theories, Lee developed a concept of martial arts for the individual man. This concept he later labeled Jeet Kune Do, the way of the intercepting fist. It has antecedents not only in his physical training and voluminous martial arts library (over two thousand books), but in his formal education as well (a philosophy major at the University of Washington, Seattle).

Lee also combined his martial arts expertise with his knowledge of acting skills and cinematic techniques, starring in several motion pictures: *The Big Boss, Fists of Fury, Way of the Dragon* and *Enter the Dragon.*

Bruce Lee's death plunged both martial arts and film enthusiasts into an abyss of disbelief. Out of their growing demand to know more of and about him, his *Tao of Jeet Kune Do* was published—which is now followed by BRUCE LEE'S FIGHTING METHOD.

This third in a series of volumes, which has been compiled and organized by his longtime friend, M. Uyehara, utilizes some of the many thousands of pictures from Lee's personal photo files. Uyehara is a former student of Bruce Lee.